OBSCURED REALMS

First edition. February 14, 2024.

Written by Valeria Valentine.

ISBN/SKU: 979-8-218-37538-6

Obscured Realms

Valeria Valentine

Published by Selima Media House, 2024.

Dedication

To all those navigating the labyrinth of suffering, grappling with its weighty embrace, and to the resilient hearts that stand beside them, offering unwavering love and support in their darkest hours.

This collection is dedicated to the countless souls entangled in the throes of anguish and pain, to the compassionate caregivers, and to the unwavering dedication of non-profit organizations tirelessly working to alleviate suffering.

May these haikus stand as a tribute to empathy and a reflection of shared experiences in the obscured realms of adversity.

ontents

INTRODUCTION

Valeria Valentina, the author behind "Obscured Realms: Haikus on Religion, Death, Suicide, Murder, Sorrow, and Redemption," delves into the intricate depths of human emotions, spiritual conflicts, and existential contemplations through succinct and evocative haikus. With a profound understanding of the human condition, Valeria Valentina weaves a tapestry of poignant verses that traverse the realms of despair, turmoil, and the pursuit of redemption.

With adeptness in concise expression, Valeria Valentina skillfully reveals the obscured realms of human emotions, offering readers an introspective glimpse into the intricate landscapes of the human soul.

ON DEATH

Eternal Slumber

WRETCHED SOUL, IN FLAMES,

DESCENDS TO FIERY ABYSS,

AGONY ENDURES.

Eternal Slumber

HEARTS GROW COLD AND NUMB,

IN DEATH'S EMBRACE,

LOST WHISPERS,

UNHEARD PAIN REMAINS.

Eternal Slumber

WITHIN SHATTERED WALLS,

HEART'S WHISPERS ECHO SORROW,

IN BLEAKNESS CONFINED.

Eternal Slumber

A SOUL'S FINAL BREATH,

LIFE EBBS AWAY LIKE THE TIDE,

ETERNAL SLUMBER.

VIBRANT HUES NOW FADE,

PETALS WILT, WHISPERS SOFTLY,

LIFE'S BEAUTY SURRENDERS.

ON MURDER

AMIDST THE BLEAKNESS,

MALEVOLENCE HOLDS ITS SWAY,

GUIDING DOWNWARD FALL.

DARKNESS EMBRACES,

SATAN'S LOVE

A TREACHEROUS TRAP,

SOUL CONSUMED IN FLAMES.

\-

LOST IN SHADOWS' DEPTH,

TEMPTATION'S VENOMOUS KISS,

SOUL'S DEMISE FORETOLD.

SILENT SCREAMS ECHO,

INNOCENT LIVES EXTINGUISHED,

GENOCIDE'S HORROR.

IN DARKNESS, CRUEL PAIN,

TORTURE'S

RELENTLESS GRASP REIGNS,

SILENT SCREAMS UNHEARD.

ON SUICIDE

HEAVY HEARTED SOUL,

SEEKING SOLACE IN THE VOID,

SILENT FINAL ACT.

DARKNESS CONSUMES HOPE,

FADING WITH EACH PASSING DAY,

FINAL CHOICE IS MADE.

Scarlet Relief

A SHARP BLADE IN HAND,

RED DROPLETS STAIN

PALE SKIN'S EDGE,

PAIN BRINGS BRIEF RELIEF.

DARKNESS OVERWHELMS,

DESPERATE HEART SEEKS ESCAPE,

SILENT EXHALE FADES.

EPHEMERAL PEAK,

LIFE'S ZENITH, A FLEETING SPARK,

CHOOSE END OVER PAIN.

ON RELIGION

Veiled Hypocrisy

PIOUS WORDS SPOKEN,

DEEDS BETRAY TRUE INTENTIONS,

HYPOCRISY'S VEIL.

Veiled Hypocrisy

PRAYERS ON THEIR LIPS,

DEEDS STAINED

WITH INSINCERITY,

HYPOCRISY REIGNS.

LYING CHRISTIANS STRAY,

HOLLOW WORDS

THAT LEAD ASTRAY,

FAITH'S PATH FADES AWAY.

PREACHER'S SOLEMN VOW,

DARKNESS MASKS

A VIOLENT DEED,

SANCTITY BETRAYED.

LIPS PRAISE, HEARTS DISTANT,

FAITH'S VENEER

CLOAKS INDIFFERENCE,

HOLLOW DEVOTION.

ON SORROW

SILENT TEARS CASCADE,

HEART'S ACHE

ECHOES THROUGH THE VOID,

LOSS PAINTS DUSK'S SORROW.

In Mourning's Embrace

MOMENTS HELD SO DEAR,

RELUCTANT TO BID FAREWELL,

TIME'S EMBRACE, TOO SWIFT.

HEARTS WEEP IN SILENCE,

SILENT ECHOES OF FRIENDSHIP,

FRIENDS DEPART, GRIEVES SOUL.

GLIMPSE OF GREATNESS FADES,

RELUCTANT STEPS

TOWARD THE NEW,

PAST'S EMBRACE LINGERS.

IDENTITY FADES,

ECHOES OF SELF LOST IN MIST,

MOURNING WHAT ONCE WAS.

ON REDEMPTION

WHISPERS TO THE WIND,

PRAY

MY PAST REMAINS UNTOUCHED,

UNKNOWN, I SEEK PEACE.

INFINITE CANVAS,

BRUSH STROKES FORGE

A PORTRAIT TRUE,

IDENTITY BLOOMS.

Rebirth's Verse

FALLEN, YET RISING,

REDEMPTION

BLOOMS FROM WITHIN,

GRACE WHISPERS ANEW.

SHADOWS OF THE PAST,

ASHAMED

FOOTSTEPS MARK THE PATH,

GROWTH IN FORGIVENESS.

FROM DEPTHS, A LIFELINE,

A HAND EXTENDED IN GRACE,

RESCUE IN SILENCE.

Valeria Valentina, a prolific writer and poet, has crafted a poignant collection of haikus. As a solitary child from a broken home, she sought solace in words, her pen dancing in secrecy. A survivor of personal tumult, her haunting haikus resonate, painting glimpses of the human soul's depths, reflecting her cryptic voyage through drug-addled echoes, faith's labyrinths, and hidden battles.

Her raw haikus delve into personal struggles—battles with suicide, self-harm, and addiction to both substances and intimacy. Born from her turmoil, these verses offer an intimate glimpse into the enigmatic poet's soul, whispering truths about life's darker corners and the resilience of the human spirit *may you find redemption*